Psychic Medium Development for Beginners

Keeping it simple

A practical Guide To Your Own Intuition

Dean James Fox

Dedicated to my lovely Mum who supports me on the earth,
my Dad and Grandad James who join me from above.

"In Our Hearts and Minds

Means We Can Never Be Apart"

Forward

Thank you for purchasing my book, but most of all thank you for inviting me on your journey as you step onto your own psychic and spiritual path. You may be taking the first step or returning to a journey you started a long time ago. No matter where you are on your golden travels, it's always good to keep it simple. As you move forward, you will learn that you will never know everything and that every day is a learning curve. But this book is a basic guide to understanding the day-to-day steps of being psychic and a medium. We all develop at different stages in our life, but I believe we are born with the gifts of being psychic and mediumistic. However, the world around us conditions us and simply helps us forget how to communicate.

Dean James Fox

Content

Introduction.

Welcome to "Psychic Mediumship for Beginners" a comprehensive guide to connecting with the spirit world and psychic abilities, by the experienced Psychic Medium, Dean James Fox. If you have ever been curious about the idea of communicating with spirit or unlocking your own psychic powers but have been intimidated by the complexity of the concept, this book is tailored to address your concerns and make the process accessible to everyone.

With a lifetime of experience, Dean James Fox has witnessed the profound impact of connecting with loved ones who have passed on and how natural psychic abilities can be used every day. Mediumship and psychic abilities are not skills reserved for the select few but are natural abilities that can be developed and honed with practice. All you need is patience, curiosity, and an open mind to start using your own inbuilt psychic powers and mediumship.

In this book, we will cover the basics of mediumship, including the difference between psychics and mediums, types of mediumship, intuitive senses, and much more. Whether you are a complete beginner or someone with some prior knowledge, this book will serve as a valuable resource to take your skills to the next level.

So, if you are ready to embark on a journey of spiritual growth and discovery, this book is the perfect starting point.

A little about me Dean James Fox.

As a young child, I remember seeing and talking to spirit with the extra ability of just knowing things before they happened, but didn't we all?

As a psychic medium, I connect with the spirit world and use my psychic ability through Clairvoyance, Clairaudience, Clairsentience, Clairgustance, and Clairalience abilities. Wow, that's a lot of "Clair's" so let's keep it simple. I can see, hear, feel, taste, and smell. Alongside that, I have Claircognizance, the ability to just know things without knowing why.

As a young boy living with my family in a small house on a local authority housing estate, I first discovered my ability to communicate with the spirit world. Despite the noise that filled our home day and night, the spirits would talk to me as I listened attentively. Though initially trusting and unafraid, I eventually learned to ignore my instincts and shut out the spirits. However, my interest was reignited when I was invited to attend a mediumship class. Over the course of two years, I dedicated myself to learning and understanding how to hone my abilities. Throughout my journey, I received valuable advice from my first mediumship teacher, Veronica - if something doesn't align with your way of working, it's not for you. Today, I continue to teach and work with the understanding that everyone's abilities and experiences are unique, and it's important to trust and embrace what feels right for each individual.

This book has been designed to accompany you on your journey towards discovering your inner psychic and mediumship abilities. Whether you find yourself breezing through the exercises or struggling to grasp the concepts, it is important to remember to not push yourself too hard. These abilities should come naturally to every individual, so if it doesn't feel right for you, don't be discouraged. Keep in mind that building trust in yourself is crucial in unlocking your full potential. Don't give up on the first try, take your time, and allow yourself to grow and develop at your own pace. With patience and dedication, you will be amazed at what you can achieve. Let this guide be your companion as you embark on this golden journey towards self-discovery.

Love, Light and Trust

DJFx

Chapter 1.

Are mediums and psychics the same thing?

Many people use the words "psychics" and "mediums" and think they mean the same thing, but the difference is massive but yet so simple to understand.

To me the word "psychic" describes a wide range of senses and perceptions which exceed our usual physical senses of hearing, taste, sight, touch, and smell.

Psychics receive information about people and events from the vibrational energy of a person, place, or object. A psychic can "read a person's energy" and may perceive past, present, or future events in that person's life.

A medium communicates directly with spirits and connects in the same way as a psychic, but instead of reading the energy of the person, they read the energy of the spirit, they can do this in many ways, they may hear, taste, see, feel, and smell also known as "the Clair's" some mediums can communicate with all "the Clair's" and other just one or two.

So, the best way to describe the difference is.

"Psychics know things, Mediums are told/shown things."

What are "the Clair's"?

You may have heard the terms "clairvoyant" or "clairsentient" but what do they mean? Well let's make it nice and simple, I've already told you that some mediums can see, hear, taste, feel and smell, well over the years they have been given fancy names (that I don't often use)

It's very easy.

The term Clair comes from French "Clair" meaning "clear".

Clairvoyance.

The word Clairvoyance mean clear-seeing or your inner-vision. A lot of mediums are called clairvoyants, meaning they can see things that other cant, but to me a clairvoyant is someone who can see a communication in pictures or even a sold image in the room,

Clairaudience.

The literal translation is clear-hearing and can be described as inner-hearing, this is when the connection you are communicating with shows you through sounds, this can feel like it's inside your own mind and naked to the ear. But some people can also hear it on the "outside" in the room.

Clairsentience.

Clairsentience is also known as Clear-feeling, I would describe it as an inner sense of something that isn't physical, this is often emotions or memory triggers, it's that feeling of a sixth sense that you just know how something feels without touching it.

Clairscent.

Clairsecent is the most common "Clair" and simply means clear-smell, this is the one that most people have experienced, You smell something that you know is not in the room or area you are in.

Clairgustance.

Again, let's keep this simple, it's a unique ability to experience taste without the actual presence of food or drink.

Claircognizance.

Clear-knowing, is that feeling of knowing something without knowing why or how you have the information. This is the most used Clair for psychic readings. Many people call this Clair "Gut Feeling".

I find that when you start on your journey of development, it is not good to get bogged down by long words you don't understand. By keeping it simple and back to basics, you will create a better understanding of how you work. Ask yourself, "Do I see, hear, feel, taste, or smell?

Chapter 2.

Energy First!

All psychic and spiritual work involves energy. It is the most basic component of our life since long before the day we landed on the earth plane at birth and long after we return to spirit. Empowering your own energy is very important and you will need to understand and familiarize yourself with your own energy, as well as the energy around you. With the understanding and control of energy, we will be able to progress on your path more smoothly, gain new abilities, and understand the hidden gifts.

What is energy?

"Energy" is an unseen force that comprises the seen and unseen world around us. This is most commonly known as universal energy. Despite the lack of measurable evidence for this force, anyone who has worked with energy will have had a subjective experience.

How you would feel or see this "energy"

- An unseen force.
- A warm or tingling sensation.
- Seeing and feeling colours.
- Change of temperature.
- A change in consciousness.
- Suddenly feeling unwell.
- Seeing things move out of the corner of your eye.
- Problems with electrical items.

Just to name a few of the many ways that energy can be shown to us.

To work with energy, we need to know the basic principles to make it work.

The first thing we must do to begin working with energy is to become aware of its existence. Remember, "Energy is everywhere." Behind every object and person is an atom, and behind every atom is energy. And it can be shown in so many ways.

For example,

the energy of the sun will have a different property than the energy of water. The sun has a warm feeling, but still water will feel cool, as they move at different speeds.

Exposing yourself to certain people will make you anxious while others make you calm, even though you are a distance away from them. Again, this is the energy of the person you are feeling or being shown by the person if they know it or not.

Energy is neutral, knows no human laws or ethics. Indeed, it is intelligent but neutral. And I believe this is the most important message to remember when we are connecting with energy, our own, others, the world around us, or even the spirit world.

Exercise 1. Sensing Energy.

When starting on the path of becoming a psychic or a medium, I find this exercise the most important of all, and you will find that I talk about your own energy and the energy around you in all the exercises in this development book. Before we start working with our psychic or mediumship energies, we need to understand our own energy and the energy around us.

Own energy.

Let's keep it simple! Look at yourself in a mirror and remember how you feel when you are happy with love or the feeling of pain in grief? This is the feeling deep inside and not what you see in your own expression. Sometimes what we see is not the true feeling.

Then ask yourself, where do you usually feel it? Find that part of you that feels the emotion, whatever emotion that may be. Some people feel happy in the heart, and others get that amazing butterfly feeling in the tummy. And when it comes to grief, some may feel dizzy, while others feel sick.

That part of you is your emotion, and where you feel your emotions is where you feel YOUR OWN energy. Everyone is different, and there is no right or wrong. The more you understand your own energy, the better you will understand the messages you receive when we start working with our psychic/mediumship abilities.

Sensing Energy in the Environment.

Let's keep this simple. When we touch something, we interact with it, and we are always interacting with and touching the environment. This means we are always sensing energy. This is why we need to understand the environment around us. I don't mean the whole world or universe; I simply mean the room or area we are in at that moment in time. But remember, this is always changing because we are always moving.

Touch is connection.

Look at your feet. Are you barefoot and are your feet touching the floor, or are you wearing socks? You will feel a different sensation for each type of floor or sock you wear. You may get a vibrational sense or, as for me, it would be a sense of goosebumps, of whatever energy you feel. It can also be cold or warm, comfortable, or hard.

For example,

a rug will have a different sensation than grass or a wooden floor. So, we can say that the rug has a different energy than the grass or the wooden floor. (You want to feel with your entire body, not just the textures of the floor.) But for now, remember how your favourite room or pair of socks make you feel. This relaxed energy may be useful later in your development.

As you become better with sensing the energy of the environment, you can begin to sense the energy without having to physically touch the environment. We can walk into the room and get a feel of what the energy of the environment is like.

For example,

walking into a quiet place has a different feel, almost a peaceful feeling compared to the workplace. The workplace has a different feel than a public coffee shop. Ask yourself how you feel in the different environments, and again remember that feeling as it will become useful as you continue on your path.

We have all walked into an argument. You can feel the intensity in the air, and it is very obvious. But can you tell if an argument has happened before you even arrived? We can practice this skill so that we can also sense the subtle parts of our environment.

Practice this feeling: feel your environment physically with your feet and get a sense of the energy as you walk into different environments. We all get that gut feeling; this is the energy around you.

But keep in mind that you are merely observing and not bringing your own emotions into the mix.

Exercise 2. Creating Energy.

To help you understand how energy works and how we can interact with it, let's have a little fun and see if you can form energy.

Step One

The first thing and most important thing is to relax.

Sit comfortably with your hands resting on your thighs, palms down.

Inhale very slowly from your diaphragm, which is below your chest, and exhale slowly.

This may take a few moments, but the more in control of your breathing you are, the more control you have of your own energy.

Step Two

When you're relaxed, bring both your hands forward as if you are holding a ball with both hands.

The palms should slightly face each other. Focus all your attention on both your hands at the same time.

Stay focused and keep all your attention on your hands, you will begin to feel a warm sensation or a tingling sensation on both of your palms.

Step Three

Once you feel this change of sensation, focus your attention on this new sensation (the gap between the hands) while still sending energy to both hands. By doing this, you are intensifying the new sensation and you should feel the energy grow, and the sensation can magnify.

Step Four

Now from your hands, imagine a beam of light, like a laser, emitting out of your palms through the gap of your hands. You can also imagine a ball of light between your hands. Some people will start to see the light or a change of colour between the hands, so don't worry if you don't. What's important is feeling the energy change. As you have started to create your own energy.

The process of feeling energy can be confusing and overwhelming at first, and it's common to feel discouraged if you don't pick it up immediately. However, it's important to remember that everyone's experience with energy is unique and there's no right or wrong way to feel it. Consistency and practice are key components in building a stronger connection to your energy and the energy around you. As you continue to work on this skill, be patient with yourself and trust that you will develop your own ways of sensing and interpreting energy.

Chapter 3.

Am I Psychic?

Psychic abilities and psychic powers allow you to have perceptions beyond the physical body. But how do you know if you have psychic abilities?

Most of us have thought about this question at some point in our lives. Maybe one day you find that you have very clear intuition, another day you may experience Deja vu and at another time you experience a vivid dream or even clairvoyance.

Some of us are more psychic than others but we are all born psychics. When it comes to developing psychic abilities, we all develop at different speeds, and some can develop more than others; but we all possess the ability of being psychic with the right training and techniques.

Psychic abilities are in fact a 'kind of intelligence'; you can learn them in the same way you learn how to drive or play a musical instrument. You simply learn how to put the things in the correct order and how to understand your own feelings.

One of the most common questions in psychic development is how can you tell if what you receive, or feel is really psychic or just pure imagination?

A psychic impression is very different from the everyday feeling given from our own imagination. At first the feelings are normally random and spontaneous that often come without warning but with practice can become focused.

They show themselves in so many ways such as a gut feeling, visions, premonitions or even knowing something about someone's past without being told, you can even feel how the person is feeling, you may have been in a good mood until they walked in the room, or you get a cold shiver, and they pop into your mind.

We don't have to be sat in a dark candlelit room to receive messages, or even be with the person the message is for, and this is the reason it's hard to tell the difference between us being psychic or just our imagination. But the more you practice, the better you will understand the "psychic feeling", so you know when you are receiving messages or just overthinking.

We are all psychic in different ways, it's creating the understanding of how we work (receive information) that is the gift, the gift is not being a psychic.

So, the answer to your question is….

"Yes, we are all psychic, but some are more powerful than others."

How will the psychic impressions be shown to me?

These impressions can manifest in many ways, such as through dreams, visions, or sudden insights. Sometimes they come all at once, flooding the mind with a wealth of information, while other times they come in dribs and drabs, revealing themselves one impression at a time. No matter how they come, these impressions are powerful tools that can help us to gain insight into the world around us and to tap into our deepest levels of intuition.

Forms of impressions:

Feelings of randomness or spontaneous thoughts.

Interruption of your normal train of thought.

Persistent nagging feeling.

Strong emotions with memories behind it.

Reoccurring visions.

Seeing the same symbols over and over again such as 1111 or 1212.

Seeing and feeling colours.

Change of temperature.

Just to name a few!

Remember, the gift is understanding how you work, and you may not feel any of the above or you may have them every single day. There is no right or wrong when it comes to working with your own psychic ability.

What type of information will be shown to me?

This is a very hard question to answer but here is a list of the most common.

The past and present.

Family

Possible future plans/path

Life history

Recent life changes

Hobbies/ interests

Life lessons

Former or new relationships

This list is ever lasting.

We can also be shown things around the world from wars to disasters,

Exercise 3. The Psychic Test.

This simple test is a perfect place to start your psychic journey , but at this stage, I'm not going to explain anything .So let's get started.

What you will need.

- A friend / family member or even a stranger. (We call them the sitter)
- A black pen
- Paper
- An envelope
- You!

Step One

Ask your friend, family member, or stranger "the sitter" to draw a simple, childlike face of how they are feeling or felt that day. Ask them to make it simple: dots for eyes, one dot for the nose, and a line for the mouth.

Then, without you looking at the drawing, ask them to place it face down in the envelope on the table in front of you.

Step Two

It's time to relax.

Sit comfortably with your hands resting on your thighs, palms down.

Inhale very slowly from your diaphragm, which is below your chest, and exhale slowly.

This may take a few moments, but the more in control of your breathing you are, the more control you have over your own energy.

Step Three

Get to know yourself and the environment around you. How do you feel? What's the energy like? Is the area you are in making you feel comfortable?

Once you feel you know your own feelings and the area around you, it's now time to start the experiment.

Step Four

Focus all your energy on the envelope without touching it. In your mind, use the energy to touch the card. Some people will see a light, and others will see nothing but will feel the energy. Make a note if you see or feel anything.

Ask the energy to draw the face in your mind or ask it to make you feel the emotion of the face on the paper. Do you see a smile or feel sad? At this stage, don't worry if you don't see or feel anything, but make a note if you do.

Now it's your turn to draw a face without saying anything to the sitter, then place it face down next to the envelope.

Step Five

Place your left hand on the envelope and your right hand on your drawing.

Inhale very slowly from your diaphragm and exhale slowly.

Ask yourself do they feel the same or is there a change of anergy?

Step six

It's time to see how you did, did you manage to draw the same image, and did you feel the emotion? Open the envelope and have a look.

What did I just do?

In this exercise, we are working out how you work as a psychic. Some people are empathic, meaning they feel energy. This can be a force or an emotion, and others see energy. This can be coloured lights or pictures in the mind or in the environment around us. Many people would call this a gift, but to me, understanding how we psychically work is "the gift."

Ask yourself, did I see anything, or did I feel it? If you didn't feel anything or see anything, do the experiment again, but this time, when you get to step four, ask the energy to show you through feelings, and make a note of how you felt. Did you feel warm or cold, and did you feel happy or sad?

If you didn't feel anything, start all over again, and at step four, ask the energy to show you. Did you see colours in the room or a face in your mind? Are the colours warm or cool colours, and what do the colours make you feel? Or did you see a smiley face or a tear in an eye?

Now you have the basics, you can do this exercise using other drawings. Ask the sitter to draw a shape or place a playing card in the envelope. This exercise is a great way of understanding energy, and the more you practice, the better you will become.

Exercise 4. Psychic Colours.

Any decorator or designer will tell you that how important colour is in our lives…The colours around us can change our moods, make us more or less active, productive, amorous, or even glamorous.

So, it shouldn't be a surprise that we use colours when we work with psychic energy. In the next exercise, we will start to create our own psychic colour chart.

What you need.

- Paper
- Red pen/pencil
- Orange pen/pencil
- Yellow pen/pencil
- Green pen/ pencil
- Blue pen/pencil
- Purple pen/pencil
- Pink pen/pencil
- Black pen/pencil
- You!

Step One

Using the red pen/pencil, draw a small square on the left side of the paper and put the pen down.

Step Two

It's time to relax.

Sit comfortably with your hands resting on your thighs, palms down. Inhale very slowly from your diaphragm, which is below your chest, and exhale slowly.

This may take a few moments, but the more in control of your breathing you are, the more control you have over your own energy.

Step Three

Focus all your energy on the "Red Square" and ask yourself how that Colour makes you feel.

Step Four

Write the first three words/emotions that come to mind.

Step Five

Repeat all the steps with the other coloured pens.

Congratulations

You have just created your own basic emotion colour chart. This chart will be something that can be used as a reference when working with your psychic energy, and again, the more you use it, the easier it will become.

When you feel more comfortable, you can expand on your colour chart by adding more colours or even shades but remember to keep it simple.

Here is a colour chart for guide purposes only and I recommend taking time to create your own.

Here is an example of an expanded colour chart.

RED.

BRIGHT. Passionate, Strong, Courageous, Luck, Happiness, Richness, Excitement, Bold, Extrovert, Alive, Activation.

DARK. Fierce, Oppressive, Vindictive, Aggressive, Rage, Danger, Stop, Frustration

ORANGE.

BRIGHT. Warm Optimism, Energy, Protection, Lightness, Joy, Pleasure, Relaxed, Calm.

DARK. Ambition, Pride, Sickly, Selfishness

YELLOW.

BRIGHT. Sun, Awake, Uplifted, Learning, Balance, Inspirational, Communication

DARK. Guidance, Insecure, Loss, Irritable

GREEN.

BRIGHT. Balance, Nature, Harmony, Earth, Versatile, Clear, Judgement,

DARK- Envy, Jealousy, Betrayal, Indecision, Illness

BLUE

BRIGHT – Peace, Healing, Cool, Sympathy, Understanding, Nursing, Relaxing, Calmness, Quiet, Settled

DARK- Deep thinker, Withdrawn, Shy, Worry, Depression

PURPLE

BRIGHT- Loyal, Intuitive, Spiritual, Solitude, Mediation, Concentration

DARK- Introvert, Unbalanced, Uneasy

PINK

BRIGHT- Love, Family, Empathy, Open minded

DARK- Deep hurt, Emotion, Power

Exercise 5. It's a sign.

There are signs and symbols for almost everything in life, such as doves for peace, horseshoes for luck, flags for countries, red hearts for love, animals for star signs, and even feathers for spirit. In everyday life, we use signs and symbols to communicate with each other without the spoken word. Most symbols also evoke an emotion. Let's take the universal sign for yes. With your hand held tight in a fist, you raise your thumb up so it points to the sky. This sign can often make you feel joy or happiness, but turn it on its head, and you feel upset or uneasy.

From birth, we are shown signs and symbols that have greater meanings than just an action or even a picture. I call this the picture dictionary, and every day of our lives, we add to this magic book in our own mind.

The problem is we have become so used to using them that we forget what they mean. So, we need to take time to remind ourselves before we can use them in our psychic work. This next exercise is to make you think about what the energy is trying to show you... are you seeing a horseshoe or feeling lucky?

It's your picture dictionary and is very important to go with your own feelings.

What you need.
- Paper
- pen/pencil

Step One
On the left-hand side of the paper, write or draw the following list.

A Cat.

A horseshoe.

A gold ring.

A white bird.

A tree.

A clock.

A rainbow.

Step Two

Next to the symbol/sign, write what it means to you,

For example,

Horseshoe – Luck

Step Three

Next to the description, write the first three words or emotions that come to mind.

Horseshoe - Luck - Happy/Relaxed/Feet.

Congratulations

You have just started to create your own Picture dictionary. this dictionary will naturally evolve as you do, and every time you see something make a mental note of it or write it down.

When I say make a note

 I want you to see and feel the energy of the symbol,

Ask yourself "What was it I saw?" "What did it mean?" And "how did it make me feel?"

One sign/symbol can mean more than just one thing and will have a different meaning to me than it will to you.

The power of symbols is fascinating. They have the ability to evoke emotions, memories, and meanings that differ from person to person. What may seem like a simple image to one, can hold a significant value to another. In my case, the symbol of a red bus brought about feelings of adventure and happiness, as I reminisced my travels in London.

However, to someone else, the same symbol could hold a different significance. For example, a person who grew up taking the bus to school every day may associate the red bus with memories of childhood and routine. Or someone who is a die-hard Harry Potter fan may see the same symbol and think of the famous scene where Harry, Ron, and Hermione take the Knight Bus to escape from danger.

That's one of the most incredible things about symbols. They can hold multiple meanings and can be interpreted in different ways. They have a universal language that can be felt and understood by many, yet still hold individual significance. It's amazing how a simple image can connect us to memories, people, and experiences that mean so much to us.

It's your meaning that's important.

Exercise 6. Putting it together.

In the last three exercises, we looked at how we work as a psychic. In Exercise 3, The Psychic Test, we asked ourselves, "Did we see or feel energy?" Then, in Exercise 4, you should have started to work with colours and how they made you feel, and what that colour meant to you. In Exercise 5, you started making your very own picture dictionary. Now, it's time to put them all together.

What you will need.

- A pack of playing cards
- A black pen/pencil
- Paper

Step One

Yet again, it's time to relax.

Sit comfortably with your hands resting on your thighs, palms down.

Inhale very slowly from your diaphragm, which is below your chest, and exhale slowly.

This may take a few moments, but the more in control of your breathing you are, the more control you have of your own energy.

Step Two

Get to know yourself and the environment around you. How do you feel? What's the energy like? Is the area you are in making you feel comfortable? Once you feel you know your own feelings and the area around you, it's now time to start the experiment.

Step Three

Shuffle the pack of cards and focus all your energy on the cards. In your mind, use the energy to touch the cards. Some people will see a light, and others will see nothing but will feel the energy.

Step Four

As you focus your energy on the entire deck of cards, select a single card out of the deck and place it face down in front of you. Do not look at it. Place the rest of the deck away from you. It is important that they are not in front of you or next to the single card. The entire deck now holds your energy, and we don't want it to affect your psychic result.

Step Five.

At this stage, it is important to **Ask Questions**. This will help you stay focused and in control of the exercise.

- **Ask** the card, "What colour are you? (Red? Black?)" Write the colour down.

Tips: Remind yourself what the two colours mean to you. Look back at your colour chart.

- **Ask** the card, "What shape are you? (Heart? Diamond? Spade? Club?)" Write the shape down.

Tip: Look back at your picture dictionary. Have you seen the shape or are you drawn to anything around you?

- **Ask** the card, "What are you? (1-10? Jack? King? Queen? Ace? – 1 and ace are the same card)" Write it down.

Tip: look at your hands how many fingers do you want to hold up? Or are you seeing/ feeling a picture – make a note of what you see as this is you adding to your own picture dictionary.

Step Six

How did you do?

Don't move any other cards, just the single card that is facedown. Turn it over and let's see how you did. Did you get the colour right? Did you know if it was a heart, diamond, spade, or club? And did you get the number or picture correct?

Congratulations

If you managed to get all three correct, but if you didn't, don't worry. Let's see if the environment has impacted your reading.

At the start, I asked you to place the full deck of cards to one side, turn over the top card of the pack, and compare your results. Again, how many out of three did you get? Now do the same with the bottom card. This will show you if you need more focus and is a great "back to basics" exercise.

I recommend doing this exercise as often as you can. You will find it's great to clear the mind and very relaxing. And when you feel relaxed, you are more at one with your own energy.

Chapter 4.

Am I a Medium?

When most people think of mediums, they think of an old lady in a long flowing skirt who is a little strange, and all the children in the area dare each other to knock on the door before running away. Well, I hate to burst that bubble, but I'm not an old lady, and children are not scared of me. I'm just a normal person, the same as everyone else.

Being a medium means having the ability to connect with the spirit world. Most people have the misconception that mediums talk to "the dead," but the truth is, most mediums can't hear spirits.

There are many ways to communicate with spirits. Some people call the ways we communicate "the Clairs," but I like to keep it simple. Some mediums hear, see, feel, smell, and taste when communicating with spirits. Some mediums, like me, have the ability to do all, but most mediums can only do one or a few of "the Clairs."

There are also a few different types of medium, the mental medium and the physical medium.

A mental medium is the most common medium, someone who is able to communicate with spirit while they are conscious through seeing, hearing, feeling, smelling, or tasting.

Physical Mediumship is not as common today as it was in Victorian times and the early twentieth century. The types of Physical phenomena usually encountered are Transfiguration, Ectoplasm, Voice Trumpets, Materialization, and Apports.

I believe that every baby is born a medium, but we are conditioned through life and forget what we were born with. We are told it's odd, strange, and even scary. But with the correct training and support, we can open up what we may have closed off or start noticing things we once ignored.

So, what makes you think you could a medium?

- ### You get mental images.

One example of this is when someone is talking to you about a deceased family member, and you get a mental flash of what that person looked like without having them described to you. Or, for no reason, you see a face in your mind, just like a photo.

- ### You can smell fragrances which aren't actually present.

Have you ever walked into a room and caught a whiff of perfume or perhaps the nasty smell of a cigarette or cigar, and no one else seems to notice it?

- ### You feel like the air is suddenly full of energy that makes you feel strange.

This is one of those signs that can really make you question your sanity before you learn to understand what is happening.

- ### Seeing things move out of the corner of your eye.

Many people have experienced seeing something move out of the corner of their eye, only to turn and find that nothing is there. For mediums, this can be a more regular phenomenon than for the average person.

- **Walking into some places causes you to get a headache.**

You might feel a heaviness or other sensations, and even emotions. Sometimes you might get a headache. This can be disconcerting, even after you are accustomed to your gift, but especially in the beginning.

- **Are you afraid of the dark?**

Many mediums have had a fear of the dark at one point or another in their lives. Okay, many children have a fear of the dark.

- **tv's, radios or even lights go on and off on their own.**

This can happen at any time of the day, and many mediums may be worried about this physical interaction.

- **Is it cold in here?**

You may get a rush of cold or hot air passing by you.

- **You feel someone, or something touch you.**

You know that you are home alone, and suddenly, something strokes your hair or nips your bottom. You turn around to find no one standing behind you.

- **Did you call me?**

You hear your name being called in random places. You could be walking down the street of a town you have never been to before, and someone calls your name. Or you could be in the bath, and you hear your name being called out, so you call back only to be told no one shouted your name.

The most common questions in mediumship.

How can you tell if what you receive, or feel is really from Spirit or just pure imagination?

A mediumistic impression can feel the same as our own imagination and can be hard to interpret, but fear not, there are exercises you can do to help you and the spirit world communicate in a way you both understand. At first, the feelings are normally random and spontaneous, and often come without warning, but with practice, they can become focused.

What information will the spirit world give me?

Again this is a very hard question to answer but here is a list of the most common

The past and present.

Family.

Possible future plans/path.

Life history.

Recent life changes.

Hobbies/ interests.

Life lessons.

Former or new relationships.

How someone died.

What they looked like.

The pain they felt.

But most of all love.

The spirit world is an elusive realm where communication is often random and unpredictable. While many people hope to receive specific messages from their loved ones who have passed away, it is crucial to understand that the spirit world operates differently from the physical world. This means that the information that spirits convey to us may not always align with our expectations or desires. We must remember that spirits have limited energy and time to communicate with us, so they may not always address the topics that we want to discuss.

To establish a connection with the spirit world, it is essential to ask questions and engage in conversation. By asking spirits questions, we can guide the conversation towards the topics that matter to us while also respecting the limitations of their energy. This approach enables us to establish a more meaningful connection with the spirit world, and it increases the likelihood of receiving relevant messages from our loved ones. Overall, developing a deeper understanding of the spirit world requires patience, open-mindedness, and a willingness to embrace unexpected communication.

Setting Intention.

Before we start working with the spirit world, we have to set the intention, meaning we have to tell them and ourselves that we are ready to work. This is the correct time for them to show us they are there, and you are in control of the connection.

This also helps us control the connection and will stop random thoughts and "jumping" connections.

I think it is very important to only work with spirits when you are ready or what some would call "open." And yes, that's right, we shouldn't be open all the time. You are in control of your communication with the spirit world, not the other way around. Many people don't know if or when they are connecting. By setting this intention, you know what to be looking for. At the same time, you are telling the spirit world when they should step forward.

How do we set intention?

Intention is the crucial first step towards meaningful communication. It involves a conscious decision to reach out and connect. By opening ourselves up, what I call picking up the phone and taking it off the answering phone, we signal our willingness to engage and understand, and to create space for mutual exchange. Whether it's through a formal greeting or a moment of silent reflection, expressing our intention to blend sets the tone for a productive conversation. Some call this an opening message or a prayer, to me it's simple - it's just a few words of respect saying, "let's talk".

Some people will send a thought out to their own spirit guides, protectors or even God, but I simply feel that this "Let's talk" should be open to the divine and ever-loving spirit.

Here is a small message of intention.

Divine and ever-loving spirits,

Could the strongest and the brightest come forward to show us that we are not alone and to remind us that we may not be able to see you every day, but you live on around us? I do this with respect and expect respect in return. This is the correct time to communicate with me, and I will let you know when I have finished. This message is to remind you that I am in control of our connection. I thank you in advance with love and light.

Amen.

I know the message sounds a little strongly worded, but it's you empowering yourself, then reminding the spirit world who is in charge. It's always done with respect, but if we didn't set the intention, the spirit world would think we wanted to talk with them when we shouldn't or when we have no one to pass the message on to.

You can make your own message of intention but remember to keep it simple and always with respect to the spirit world, but most of all to yourself.

Closing off to the spirit world

The idea of closing off is again an intention of ending communication with the spirit world around us. If we didn't close off or place the phone on silent/answer phone, we would be open to communication 24 hours a day, 7 days a week, 365 days a year, and the spirit world would be trying to chat at every opportunity.

The main reasons for closing communication are:

You are in control, Its respect for yourself, Its respect for other people around you,

But most of all its, so you know when you are receiving a message and it's not just your own random thoughts,

How to close a message/ end communication until you are ready to start working again.

Divine and ever-loving spirits,

Thank you for showing me that you support my spiritual work and that you believe in me, but now I send all the light and love back to you, as I return to my normal life. I remind you that this is my time and my life, so with respect, please step back until I send the message of love and ask for communication. Once again, I thank you for your communication, with love and light.

Amen.

THIS IS THE MOST IMPORTANT MESSAGE YOU WILL EVER SEND TO SPIRIT!

If you find that spirit is around you after you have said this message, don't worry. Don't be surprised if it was you that invited them in without noticing. Did you see something and say, "what's that," or smell something and say, "who's there"?

Remember, simple words can open communication.

So, what to do if you have opened by accident,

BE STRONG!

Say to them, thank you for showing me that you are there, but with respect, this is not the correct time.

I always say, keep it simple. Make your own messages of intention but remember the spirit world will talk/show us that they are there if we want them to. It's up to you to tell them whether or when you want to listen.

Exercise 7. Seeing spirit in the room.

The word Clairvoyance means clear-seeing or your inner-vision. In this exercise, we will be looking at clear-seeing, meaning we will be trying to see the energy of the spirit world around you. I don't want to explain too much at this stage, so let's crack on. Just one tip before we start, don't be embarrassed about talking to yourself!

What you need:

- A dark room
- A candle
- Pen and paper
- A friend (sitter) or alone

Step One

Light the candle and turn the lights down or off.

Step Two

It's time to relax.

Sit comfortably with your hands resting on your thighs, palms down.

Inhale very slowly from your diaphragm, which is below your chest, and exhale slowly.

This may take a few moments, but the more in control of your breathing you are, the more control you have of your own energy. The better the connection.

Step Three

Get to know yourself and the environment around you. How do you feel? What's the energy like? Is the area you are in making you feel comfortable? Once you feel you know your own feelings and the area around you, it's now time to start the experiment.

Step Four

Set Intention

Divine and ever-loving spirits,

Please let the strongest and the brightest come forward to show us that we are not alone and to remind us that we may not be able to see you every day, but you live on around us. I do this with respect and expect respect in return. This is the correct time to communicate with me, and I will let you know when I have finished. This message is to remind you that I am in control of our connection. I thank you in advance with love and light.

Amen.

Step Five

Look directly at the candle and say out loud,

"Please use the energy of this candle to show me that you are there. Move the candle's flame for me."

Keep asking the spirit world to show themselves by moving the candle's flame. Don't lose focus.

Once you feel the energy or the flame change, move on to the next step.

Step Six

Now stare at a dark corner of the room and let your eyes rest and focus, this will take a few moments.

Then out loud say,

"Please move the light from the candle to make a flash of light in the dark. This is you showing me your energy, not you moving the candle. Use my energy, your energy and the candle's energy to show me you are with me."

(You may see movement out of the corner of your eye or a full flash in the room.)

Don't worry if you don't see anything the first time you do this, but we can still communicate with spirit.

Step Seven

Let's talk!

Stare at the candle again and say,

"Thank you for showing me you are there. Now let's talk. Please move the candle flame to the left for yes and to the right for no."

Now it's time to find out who we are talking to but remember to keep it simple.

"Are you a man? Move the flame to the left for yes and to the Right for no."

"Are you a woman? Move the flame to the left for yes and to the right for no."

"Are we related? Move the flame to the left for yes and to the right for no."

Remember, when asking questions, they can only answer yes or no, so keep it simple. Write the full communication down as it's very hard to keep track of what you have asked.

Step Eight

It's time to close the communication.

Divine and ever-loving spirits,

Thank you for showing me that you support my spiritual work and that you believe in me, but now I send all the light and love back to you, as I return to my normal life. I remind you that this is my time and my life, so with respect please step back until I send the message of love and ask for communication.

Once again, I thank you for your communication, with love and light,

Amen.

What did you just do?

You Just created a connection by seeing moving energy. This is a basic start to seeing spirit, but as you move on, you will move away from the candle by concentrating on the dark corner of the room. Then start to ask the spirit world to show itself in the room. Don't worry if this never happens, as it takes a lot of the spirit's energy to show itself, and to me, it is not the best form of communication.

Remember, you are in control, and by opening and closing off to spirit, you are in charge.

"I believe in spirit, because it believes in me."

Exercise 8. Seeing Spirit with the Inner-vision.

As we now know, the spirit world is amazing and can work in so many ways. In this exercise, we will be looking at your inner-vision, meaning we will be trying to see and connect with spirit in our mind's eye, and the way we do this is in pictures or moving images. The images can feel like your own thoughts or that strange feeling at the back of your mind, or even like your own memory of your own past.

If you are following the exercise in this book step by step, you will have already started to understand how we can receive messages by picture (see Exercise 5, it's a sign). If you have jumped a few pages, I recommend going back and reading the exercise before you continue. You should have now started to make your own picture dictionary, and the more you work with spirit, the larger your dictionary.

In this exercise, we will be seeing if we can describe spirit, and I recommend not doing this on your own, not because it's scary or hard, just because there is no evidence in your own message. At this stage, we are giving you the tools to connect and to create trust in yourself.

What you need:

- A friend (sitter)
- A pen and paper
- You!

Before you start, ask your friend not to tell you too much. They should sit still and only answer "Yes," "No," or "maybe." So, let's begin.

Step One

It's time to relax.

Sit comfortably with your hands resting on your thighs, palms down.

Inhale very slowly from your diaphragm, which is below your chest, and exhale slowly.

This may take a few moments, but the more in control of your breathing you are, the more control you have of your own energy. The better the connection.

Step Two

Get to know yourself and the environment around you. How do you feel? What's the energy like? Is the area you are in making you feel comfortable? Once you feel you know your own feelings and the area around you, it's now time to start the experiment.

Step Three

Set Intention

Divine and ever-loving spirits,

Please let the strongest and the brightest come forward to show us that we are not alone and to remind us that we may not be able to see you every day, but you live on around us. I do this with respect and expect respect in return. This is the correct time to communicate with me, and I will let you know when I have finished. This message is to remind you that I am in control of our connection. I thank you in advance with love and light.

Amen.

Step four

As you sit across from your friend, ask yourself, do you feel a change of energy? Once you feel a small change in yourself or the room around you, you may begin this exercise. At this stage, don't worry about who you are connecting to in spirit. Simply follow the steps.

Step by step, ask the following questions to the spirit world (not your friend; that would be cheating) and without thinking, write down the first thing you see.

There is no wrong or right here. Please don't show or tell your friend what you are seeing. Just write it down.

- "Show me in my mind what shoes you are wearing." Write the first thing down.
- "Show me in my mind what colour eyes you have." Write down the colour.
- "Show me in my mind a place." Write down the place you see. You may know the place, or you may have to describe it.
- "Show me in my mind what colour hair you have." Remember, some people don't have hair.
- "Show me in my mind a member of my family." Just write the first thing you see down.
- "Show me in my mind a picture from my symbol dictionary." Just write down the symbol.

Now check your list. Did you manage to get answers to all the questions? Don't worry if you didn't; just write down the first thing that comes to mind.

- Did you see men's shoes or ladies' heels?
- What kind of shoes are they?
- What colour eyes did you see?
- Where did they show you as a place?
- Did you get the colour of hair?
- Who is the family connection?
- What symbol did you see?

Step Five

Now it's time to talk with your friend. While looking at the paper in front of you, tell your friend what you saw.

Tell your friend the place, eyes, and feet you saw and ask them if they understand someone in spirit who would wear shoes like that, who would also have the eye colour you saw, then ask if they could be connected to the place in your vision. (The place could also be a connection for your friend.)

Ask your friend if they think they know who you are connecting with.

Now look at the member of the family you saw in your mind's eye,

Was it dad, mum, gran, grandad, sister? This is part of your picture dictionary, i.e., if you saw dad, ask the sitter (your friend) if the connection is their dad or are they on dad's side.

Now look at the symbol you saw, what did it mean to you? This is the message from spirit to your friend, don't worry if you don't understand the symbol. It could be a secret message for your friend. But don't be shy, have trust in yourself and spirit.

Step Six

It's time to close the communication,

Divine and ever-loving spirits,

Thank you for showing me that you support my spiritual work and that you believe in me, but now I send all the light and love back to you, as I return to my normal life. I remind you that this is my time and my life, so with respect, please step back until I send the message of love and ask for communication. Once again, I thank you for your communication, with love and light.

Amen.

Congratulations

You just received a message from your inner vision, but don't worry if you didn't manage to see anything. It takes a lot of trust in yourself that may only come with time, and this is the reason we don't do this exercise on our own. We need others to confirm your connection.

"I believe in spirit, because it believes in me."

Exercise 8. Hearing the spirit world.

The word Clairaudience's literal translation is clear-hearing and can also be described as inner-hearing. This is when the connection you are communicating with shows you through sounds. When we talk about hearing spirit, it's not the same as sitting with friends over coffee chatting about the day or picking up the phone at work to speak to colleagues in London. It's not as simple as that.

It takes a lot of energy for the spirit world to show you with sound that they are in the room. It's easier for them to chat/talk and show in our minds. I call this spirit to spirit.

So, in this exercise, we are going to concentrate on the inner-hearing (spirit to spirit) when we hear spirit in our own minds. It can feel like we are talking to ourselves or even having random thoughts, so it takes a lot of trust. Just say/write what you hear or your first thought that springs to mind. The more you do this, the more you will understand when it's you thinking or when it's spirit working spirit to spirit. Again, this is the main reason we have a friend/sitter so they can give feedback as you give evidence of spirit connection. Other than that, who's to say you're not talking to yourself?

What you need:
- Pen and paper
- A friend (sitter)
- You!

Step One

Sit across from the sitter in a quiet room, turn all TVs, radios, phones, or anything that will make noise off. Even a ticking clock can be a distraction.

Step Two

It's time to relax.

Sit comfortably with your hands resting on your thighs, palms down.

Inhale very slowly from your diaphragm, which is below your chest, and exhale slowly.

This may take a few moments, but the more in control of your breathing you are, the more control you have of your own energy. The better the connection.

Step Three

Get to know yourself and the environment around you. How do you feel? What's the energy like? Is the area you are in making you feel comfortable? Once you feel you know your own feelings and the area around you, it's now time to start the experiment.

Step Four

Set intention.

Divine and ever-loving spirits,

Please let the strongest and the brightest come forward to show us that we are not alone and to remind us that we may not be able to see you every day, but you live on around us. I do this with respect and expect respect in return. This is the correct time to communicate with me, and I will let you know when I have finished. This message is to remind you that I am in control of our connection. I thank you in advance with love and light.

Amen.

Step Five

As you sit across from your friend, ask yourself if you feel a change of energy. Once you feel a small change in yourself or the room around you, you may begin this exercise. At this stage, don't worry about who you are connecting to in spirit.

Step by step, ask the following questions to the spirit world (not your friend, that would be cheating) and without thinking, write down the first thing you hear. There is no wrong or right here. Please do not show or tell your friend what you are seeing, just write it down.

- *"Tell me in my mind – please give me a name."*

Write down the first name you hear (even if you think it's just you thinking it).

- *"Tell me in my mind – please give me a song that connects to you or the person I'm sat with."*

Write down the song or few words you hear / what first comes to mind. (Again, don't worry if you think it's just your own thoughts).

- *"Tell me in my mind – please give me a month."*

Write down the month you hear or what springs to mind.

Step Six

Now it's time to talk with your friend.

Looking at the paper in front of you and tell your friend what you heard.

- Can your friend/the sitter connect to the name (upstairs – spirit world, downstairs– earth or in the middle meaning they are ready to take their transition to the spirit world)?

- Do they have a connection to the song? Or do they understand the message of the lyrics? Sometimes the song is what was played at a funeral, wedding or even that one special song that means the world. It can also be the message of the lyrics that is important,

    i.e., the wind beneath my wings, which could mean you or they were the main support when needed.

- Is the month important to the sitter or the spirit world? Is the month special for birthdays or funerals?

- Is the number a date that is connected to the month or just one that is special to the sitter or spirit world?

- What was the random sound? It may mean nothing to the sitter, it may form part of your sound dictionary, and so what did the random sound mean to you?

Step Seven

It's time to close the communication,

Divine and ever-loving spirits,

Thank you for showing me that you support my spiritual work and that you believe in me, but now I send all the light and love back to you, as I return to my normal life. I remind you that this is my time and my life, so with respect, please step back until I send the message of love and ask for communication.

Once again, I thank you for your communication, with love and light.

Amen.

Congratulations.

You just received a message from your inner ear. At this stage, you shouldn't worry if you got one word correct or all correct. The fact is, you're starting to understand yourself and how Spirit can work with you. And don't worry if you didn't manage to hear anything; it takes a lot of trust in yourself that may only come with time. This is the reason we don't do this exercise on our own; we need others to confirm your connection.

"I believe in spirit, because it believes in me."

Exercise 10. feeling the spirit world.

Clairsentience means 'clear-feeling'. It is perhaps the most down-to-earth of all the Clair. Most people use clairsentience daily. To give a common example: you may experience a feeling of discomfort or great joy, or within seconds the feelings change without warning.

When working with spirit, there are many ways we feel spirit:

Gut feeling

Gut feelings are strong emotional responses that feel almost physical – for example, a feeling of dread or a feeling of excitement. That feeling that something did not or will not end well that gives you a sinking feeling. Or an uplifted, excited feeling in the gut could mean you're on the right track. When working with spirit, use that gut feeling in your message alongside what you are being shown or hearing.

Empathy

Empathy is the ability to pick up on the feelings of other people and know what it is like to be that person. Empathy can be a double-edged sword. It allows you to put yourself in other people's shoes. But be warned, you must take control of this gift from day one. "Why?" you ask. Well, if you're an empath, you can be like a sponge, absorbing and feeling emotions that aren't your own. But you can have that same strong feeling. Ask yourself, do you ever experience overwhelming negative feelings that seem to have no cause?

Then you could be feeling someone else's feelings. This feeling can be psychic (on the earth) or mediumistic (given from spirit).

Physical Sensations

Clairsentience also speaks to you through sensations in your body, from small signs like tickling or pressure to painful signs that feel like your own problems.

Clairsentience can be one of the strongest gifts. You may receive impulses all the time through physical sensations or just when you're tuning into spirit doing a reading. Most people get a strong tingling sensation on both sides of their head, but others just get a little tickle down the back of the neck. Some use this as a sign when spirit has stepped up to talk. But if you're like me, you will also feel the pain of how the spirit passed or just the everyday pain they felt on the earth. It's up to you if you let the spirit world show you this form of connection, and just a few words can stop it, so don't panic. You have the power to stop the feeling, and it's very simple.

Just say, "Is this feeling mine or being shown to me? If it's being shown to me, take it off now." If the feeling is removed, then it's not yours. But if it keeps being shown to you, say the words again. If it continues, then it's more than likely to be your own feelings/pain.

If you never want to work this way, simply say, "Thank you for showing me, but take it off and never work with me like this again. I am in control of our connection." You really have to be strong. The spirit world will respect you as you respect them.

So, let's get down to the exercise. You can do this on your own, but you will need a photograph given by a friend in an envelope of someone in the spirit world. I recommend doing this exercise with a sitter.

What you need:

- A friend (sitter)
- A pen and paper
- A photograph of someone in the spirit world connected to the sitter. (do not look at the photo yet)
- You!

Step One

It's time to relax.

Sit comfortably with your hands resting on your thighs, palms down.

Inhale very slowly from your diaphragm, which is below your chest, and exhale slowly.

This may take a few moments, but the more in control of your breathing you are, the more control you have of your own energy. The better the connection.

Step Two

Get to know yourself and the environment around you. How do you feel? What's the energy like? Is the area you are in making you feel comfortable? Once you feel you know your own feelings and the area around you, it's now time to start the experiment.

Step Three

Set intention.

Divine and ever-loving spirits,

Please let the strongest and the brightest come forward to show us that we are not alone and to remind us that we may not be able to see you every day, but you live on around us. I do this with respect and expect respect in return. This is the correct time to communicate with me, and I will let you know when I have finished. This message is to remind you that I am in control of our connection. I thank you in advance with love and light.

Amen.

Step Four

Ask a friend to show you the picture. Look into the person's eyes in the photo and tune into their energy.

When you feel a small change, move on to the next step.

Step Five

Ask yourself, how do they feel at the moment of the photo being taken? If this is the first time you have consciously used your clairsentience, you may just pick up on a basic negative or positive vibe.

Write down as much as you can as you describe the person through feelings. Do they make you happy or sad? What kind of person do you think they are?

If you're not already feeling anything, say *"Please show me the feeling you felt at the time of this photo being taken."*

Step Six

Ask the spirit world to show you something on your body that is a feeling the spirit felt. This can be at the time of passing or everyday life.

"Please show me by making me feel a sensation. This can be on my body but only for 1 second. At this stage, only show me a tingle, not pain."

Remember, you are in control. And if you don't like the feeling, just say, *"Thank you for showing me, but take it off. I am in control of our connection."*

Write what you felt down in as much detail as you can, but don't show the sitter (your friend) just yet.

Step Seven

Ask the spirit for a message, look at the photo again, and say, *"Give me a feeling you wish to pass on."* Then, write down what you feel.

Step Eight

Now it's time to talk with your friend (sitter).

Looking at the paper in front of you, tell the sitter what you felt step by step.

How did you feel when you first saw the photograph? Can the sitter understand the information?

Did you feel any focus on a part of your body? Explain to the sitter what you felt and ask them if they understand why.

When you asked for a message, how did you feel? Give as much information as you can to the sitter. This could be the feeling they have been waiting for.

Step Nine

It's time to close the communication,

Divine and ever-loving spirits,

Thank you for showing me that you support my spiritual work and that you believe in me, but now I send all the light and love back to you, as I return to my normal life. I remind you that this is my time and my life, so with respect, please step back until I send the message of love and ask for communication.

Once again, I thank you for your communication, with love and light.

Amen.

How did you do?

There is an amazing feeling of power when working this way with spirit, but it can also be very confusing. Remember to ask questions, not just wait for feelings. The more you ask, the more you will feel, and the more you will understand how you work.

So, give yourself a pat on the back. You have probably been more focused on this task than any of the others. If you didn't feel you did well, look at what you just did again in more detail. You are just starting on the path of working with spirit. Take time to understand your own feelings. This is what the spirit world will draw from. The more you do this exercise, the better you will become. As we are working with feelings, you are bound to feel emotional.

"I believe in spirit, because it believes in me."

Exercise 11. More than one "Clair"

Well well well, you have made it to the last exercise in my book, so a massive congratulations for getting so far and not giving up on yourself. But now the real work begins. This is where we start to put everything together, so without me explaining what we are going to do, let's get on with it!

Before you start the next exercise, you should already be getting ready to work!

What should you be doing?

You should already be preparing yourself to work. In all the exercises, the first few steps have been the same and you should now be doing this without thinking.

You should be relaxed, checked your environment, and set intention. The steps not only prepare you for work but also inform the spirit world you are ready and waiting. But don't worry, I will give you the steps again.

What you need:

- A friend (sitter)
- A pen and paper
- You!

Step One

It's time to relax.

Sit comfortably with your hands resting on your thighs, palms down.

Inhale very slowly from your diaphragm, which is below your chest, and exhale slowly.

This may take a few moments, but the more in control of your breathing you are, the more control you have of your own energy. The better the connection.

Step Two

Get to know yourself and the environment around you. How do you feel? What's the energy like? Is the area you are in making you feel comfortable? Once you feel you know your own feelings and the area around you, it's now time to start the experiment.

Step Three

Set intention.

Divine and ever-loving spirits,

Please let the strongest and the brightest come forward to show us that we are not alone and to remind us that we may not be able to see you every day, but you live on around us. I do this with respect and expect respect in return. This is the correct time to communicate with me, and I will let you know when I have finished. This message is to remind you that I am in control of our connection. I thank you in advance with love and light.

Amen.

Step Four

Sit across from the sitter and stay focused, ask the sitter to only reply yes, no or unsure. This is important so you can stay focused. If the sitter says no or unsure, still write it down, as this information could be evidence the sitter just doesn't know. So don't be put off.

Step Five

Once you feel a change of energy around you, ask the spirit world the following questions, write down the answer and how you got this information,

Example:

"I have a man with me (felt) he has black boots (saw)."

Then, after you have written them down, ask the sitter if they understand the information. YES, NO, OR UNSURE!

I will prompt you when to ask the sitter. Remember to ask the spirit world with your mind (in your head).

- *"Are you a man or woman?"*

Write down the first thing that pops into your mind and how you got the answer (saw, felt, heard).

- *"What shoes do you wear? Please show me your feet."*

Write down the first thing that pops into your mind and how you got the answer (saw, felt, heard).

- *"Are you young or old?"*

Write down the first thing that pops into your mind and how you got the answer (saw, felt, heard).

- *"Are you related to the person in front of me?"*

Write down the first thing that pops into your mind and how you got the answer (saw, felt, heard).

- *"Please show me a member of my family or a friend I know, so I know how you connect to the person in front of me."*

Write down the first thing that pops into your mind and how you got the answer (saw, felt, heard).

TELL YOUR FRIEND WHO YOU HAVE A CONNECTION WITH.

- Do you have a man or woman with you?
- How did you see their feet or shoes?
- Are they old or young?
- Are they a friend or related to you?
- They are showing me *….. That makes me think they are your *….. or connected to them.

-

Can they understand this person in spirit so far? (Write down the answers given by the sitter)

Ask the spirit world with your mind (in your head).

- *"Please show me an illness that connects to you or the person in front of me."*

Write down the first thing that pops into your mind and how you got the answer (saw, felt, heard).

- *"Please give me a name that connects to you or the sitter."*

Write down the first thing that pops into your mind and how you got the answer (saw, felt, heard).

- *"Please show me a place that connects to you or the sitter."*

Write down the first thing that pops into your mind and how you got the answer (saw, felt, heard).

- *"Please show me a colour from my picture dictionary."*

Write down the first thing that pops into your mind and how you got the answer (saw, felt, heard).

TELL YOUR FRIEND

Ask your friend if they understand the illness or the area of the body you are drawn to. Then, ask if they understand how it connects to the spirit or themselves. Ask the place and if they understand why it's being shown. Next, tell the sitter what the colour was, then look at your own colour dictionary and explain what it means to you. Finally, can they understand the information so far? (Write down the answers given by the sitter)

Ask the spirit world with your mind (in your head)

- *"Please show me what kind of person you are."*

Write down the first thing that pops into your mind and how you got the answer (saw, felt, heard).

- *"Can you please give me a song that connects to you or the person in front of me?"*

Write down the first thing that pops into your mind and how you got the answer (saw, felt, heard).

- *"Why are you here and do you have a message to pass on?"*

Write down the first thing that pops into your mind and how you got the answer (saw, felt, heard).

TELL YOUR FRIEND

- What kind of personality did they have?

Ask the sitter if they understand the song, does it connect to the sitter or spirit?

Now this is the important part of the reading,

- Why have they come?
- What's the message from spirit?
- How did it make you feel?
- Can they understand the information so far?

(Write down the answers given by the sitter)

Step Six

It's time to close the communication,

Divine and ever-loving spirits,

Thank you for showing me that you support my spiritual work and that you believe in me, but now I send all the light and love back to you, as I return to my normal life. I remind you that this is my time and my life, so with respect, please step back until I send the message of love and ask for communication.

Once again, I thank you for your communication, with love and light.

Amen.

How did you do?

It's now time to look at how you just connected with spirit. You should have made a side note to each of the 12 questions you just asked, saying if you saw, heard, or felt the answers.

How many times out of 12 did you write down?

Saw?

Heard?

Felt?

By doing this task, you are being shown the strongest Clair you work with at the moment.

If you saw more of the answers to the questions, I would say you are more Clairvoyant.

If you heard (in your mind or in the room) more of the answers, I would say you are more Clairaudient.

And if you felt more of the answers at this stage, I would say you're more Clairsentient.

But this is not set in stone. The way we work can change every day and with every spirit, so it's a good idea to make a note of how you receive messages. This will help you know the areas you are strong at, or you wish to work on.

"I believe in spirit, because it believes in me."

Chapter 5.

Smelling and tasting.

You may have noticed that I haven't set an exercise for Clairscent or Clairgustance? This is not because they are not important, but I just feel that they are the easiest to understand out of all the "clairs" and the easiest to take control of. How many times have we walked into a room and noticed the strange smell, smelled flowers or sweet perfume? Now you have started to understand the main way you connect with spirit; you can start to insert questions that will be based on these Clairs.

The simplest are:

Smell: *"Please show me a smell that is connected to you."*

You may smell roses or even get the not so nice smell of a nursing home or even worse!

Taste: *"Please show me the food you like to eat or that is connected to you."*

You may see an image or a memory, so reword the question. "Please let me taste what you have just shown me." Be careful when you say this; you really don't want to ask this just after smelling a nursing home!

Chapter 6.

Let The Journey begin.

As you grow and explore your psychic and mediumship gift, you will find yourself expanding not only as a human but also as a stronger spirit. When I reopened the door on my own psychic and spiritual path, I realized that we are all the same, just a form of natural energy burning at different speeds.

Life may not be perfect, and sometimes we think we can't move on with our day-to-day or even our lives, but every time you feel this way, remind yourself that you are your own energy. Take time and refuel.

Take this book, for example. I started writing to show others how easy it is to connect to the spirit world and understand your own psychic ability but finished it knowing I am empowering people to follow their own spirit.

I often say,

"I believe in spirit because it believes in me, but when did we forget to believe or trust in ourselves?"

"I believe in you".

I would like to thank everyone who has joined me on my own journey, and a little extra thank you to everyone who has supported my psychic/spiritual journey. I am me because of you, whether on the earth or in spirit. You are and always will be part of my life.

Love, Light and Belief. DJFx

"In our Hearts and Minds,
Means We Can Never Be Apart"

Printed in Great Britain
by Amazon